TOILET
A BASIC GUIDE

The N

Andy B & Jamien Bailey

BB

www.booksbyboxer.com

Published in the UK by
Books By Boxer, Leeds, LS13 4BS
© Books By Boxer 2014
All Rights Reserved

ISBN: 9781909732285

Using the toilet, the most basic everyday need in everyone's life, has been couched in inhibitions for a long time. The Victorians wouldn't speak of it, the Edwardians used to disguise it, the Americans would refer to it only using the euphemism of "restroom".

Words like W.C.,Crapper, (relating to Thomas Crapper, the alleged inventor of the water closet) could not be used.

When Thomas Crapper first displayed his sanitary ware in public in late 19th century England, genteel ladies would literally faint at the sight of such glaring examples of 'filth'.

He was pilloried by polite society for daring to suggest that such unhygienic appliances could be positioned inside a house.

Now things have changed - or have they?
Toileting is still an emotive subject and the
art of correct toileting is still important for
some. This book is here to help.
**Read, before you go to avoid embarrassing
mistakes!**

So, with this essential book under your arm,
walk proudly to the loo and fire your way

through our whistle-stop tour of the Poo's (and the Poo-Poo's) of one of life's most natural and sacred acts!

And, as with anything to do with poo - **avoid putting your foot in it!**

It is important, in the subtle world of 'poo', that you don't make a boo boo of the job, a faux pas that could leave you out in the cold socially, (especially if you have an outside loo) and important that you do everything by the book...

...the toiletiquette book that is.

Getting Down To Basics

Before you take to the throne, you must be sure that you're ready to assume the correct position and best approach to the job.

As they say in the army...

...**P**roper **P**reparation **P**revents **P**iss **P**oor **P**erformance!

(That's 6 **P**'s one after the other, more than enough for one visit!)

The Correct Position

The correct position to adopt of course is the sitting down one. Sounds obvious, but think of those times you've found shoe prints on the seat. It is very bad manners to stand on the seat and squat regardless of religious and cultural reasons or the fact that the public loo has no seat. **Always face outwards.**

The Approach

The usual method is to drop your undergarments and back yourself towards the seat. Always check for snakes and small furry animals that may be lurking just above the water line.

Keep The Toilet Tidy

It's a simple philosophy that should always be followed but here are some key rules:

- Throw a bit of toilet roll into the bowl before you begin - this will aid in the prevention of unsightly skid marks.
- Don't flick bogies at the toilet door – I mean, come on, you're sat right next to a roll of tissue!
- Don't graffiti – it may be the best joke ever but trust us – the cleaners won't find it funny!

NEVER PUT ANYTHING DOWN THE PAN THAT HASN'T BEEN EATEN FIRST!

Be Thrifty

Be green. Never use more than 3 sheets together on the first wipe, then 2 on the second and 1 only for subsequent wipes.

WARNING: Check the quality of the paper first to prevent the worst of all possible toilet experiences...

...THE BREAKTHROUGH!

Be Prepared For The Unexpected
(Guide for the elderly)

Getting older, one finds that 'getting caught out' can become a problem. A propensity to pee urgently can come in a flash and you may be on a bus, a long walk or even on the job and not be able to get to the toilet in time. Therefore be prepared and follow these 2 simple rules.

Never pass a toilet without going in.

Be Equipped

Always keep a few sheets of lavatory paper tucked into your handbag or wallet for that occasion when the roll runs out and you are still 'on a roll'!

It'll be much more comfortable than using some old newspaper and much cheaper than using your folding money in desperation.

Reading on The Toilet

For many, this activity is the highlight of the day; a chance to repose in quiet comfort, without interruptions and enjoy a few chapters of your book, work out the crossword or read latest news.

Choice of reading material is important. Broadsheet newspapers are not suitable for reading in the loo because you generally do not have enough room to turn the pages, so stick to the tabloids. Newspapers have the added advantage of being useful in case of paper shortage emergencies.

Books are an ideal toilet companion but don't take a book in with you that is too large as this can become a bit unwieldy. Do not take a really exciting book as you could be in there for hours and you might get cold or piles or worse. A scary book might make you open your bowels pre-emptively with possible disastrous consequences.

The best choice of books for the lavatory are books with useless bits of information and with dubious humour, a book without intelligence and no real structure, a useless book that you can pick up and put down at whim, in fact... **a bit like this book!**

The Toiletiquette of Reading on the Toilet

It is important to be hygienic and the essential toiletiquette point is:

You must put down your book before you do the "paperwork" and then, don't pick it up again until you have washed your hands. The dangers of this are quite obvious. Books are notorious for hoarding germs and any poo contamination can be quickly passed on by the book to others, including yourself. However, this could be a subtle way of revenge by passing a freshly contaminated book onto people you don't like.

"Mmm, the boss usually nabs my paper in the lunch break?"

The Science of Pooing

Normally, the laws of Newton apply.

As Shakespeare once said *"Waste not thy time in windy argument but let the matter drop."* And, right verily, the matter normally droppeth...

...but that is not always the case.

"One small step for man, one giant heap for mankind"

BOLDLY GO

POOP DECK LAUNCH PAD

(don't use when in the spacestation)

How To Get Your Own Back...

...pee into the wind!

Modern Conveniences

You might say that an ideal toilet cubicle would include some of these things: **mini bar, HD TV, qualified masseuse!**

However, realistically - we're lucky if we get one of these things: **seat, bog roll, lock, door!**

In the Seat of Battle

Many people don't realise it but the shape of a toilet seat is thought by some to greatly affect **pooing performance**.

So here's our quick guide to some of the more common shapes...

The Bevelled Surface

As aesthetically pleasing as this design is, its slope towards the centre serves to push the cheeks together and thus, can actually restrict pooing performance.

The Flat Surface

Probably the most prevalent of seat shapes and one that manages to achieve a good level of cheek spread, if not the best.

If it was good enough for the Romans, it's good enough for us.

Toilet Seat Material

This can be important for the enjoyment of a pleasant pooing experience, a factor in completing a satisfactory job in comfort and sensory exuberance.

Plastic

The most popular and user friendly seat material. It's very functional, cleans up well, and warms up nicely after a few minutes. Prone to breaking by heavyweights but cheap to replace.

Wood

By far the warmest seat and feels good under bum. Probably harbours a few germs in the crevices but otherwise a good choice. It's popular with royalty, mahogany being a favourite in the throne room, and with oak and beech, makes a right royal flush.

Stainless Steel

Popular with street toilets but not particularly comfortable. These seats will freeze the nethers off you and give you dreadful piles if used regularly on cold mornings.

Porcelain

Very posh, the original, but still a cool (in the frozen sense) poo.

There is also a feeling that you might be better sitting on the rim under the seat

The Cushioned Toilet Seat
This may seem comfortable at first but cheek spreadage is a bit of a lottery.
There are also hygienic issues for fidgety pooers.
Alongside this, when you come to stand up, you may find that cheek-to-seat adhesion has been achieved!

The Transparent Seat Filled with Seashells, Barbed Wire or Fruit

Absolutely naff.
In the solemn, ritualistic confinements of the temple of thunder, creating an ambience of anticipation in the build up to the serene, exquisite joys of a good dump - this adds

nothing!

It's a distraction, an abomination to those who enjoy the delights of a long sojourn in the bog. And finally…

A Sloped Surface

I would suggest that a toilet seat surface that slopes away from the centre is arguably the best for cheek spreadability and, therefore, could be regarded as the seat most likely to achieve optimum pooing performance!

The Toiletiquette Of Remaining Anonymous

- Are you a secret secreter ?
- Do you flush with embarrassment if caught in the khasi?
- Are you a covert crimper, a private pooper or a shy shitzter?

Then whoopee doo, this section's for you...

Skip to the Loo!

The quicker you get to the cubicle, the less chance there is of being noticed.

Beware, move too quickly on those wet toilet floors and it could make toileting very difficult indeed...

Shiny Floors

This can be particularly embarrassing for ladies. There are some exquisite toilets where tiled floors are polished with such diligence, they virtually become a mirrored surface. Always beware who may be in the next cubicle to you. Men have been known to hover around these loos in various disguises; wig and make-up for the better looking ones and heavy religious 'cover all' clothing for the ugly fat old perverts (U.F.O's). Be aware and cover up quick if you see a pair of lascivious eyes staring up at you from under the door or partition.

It's All Give and Take in The Gents...
(Erm, it's not exactly what it sounds like)
Remember to afford others the same anonymity and the respect you would expect to receive, in the toilet.

Cubicle to cubicle conversations are to be discouraged and talking across the urinal is not generally advised, especially with strangers in a strange loo.

It's a Whose Shoe of Poo!

If your anonymity is to be protected, then you need to consider all of the little things that might give you away whilst you're turning one out...

Shoes are a dead giveaway, especially if you are wearing socks with your name splattered all over them. So this leaves you with few options.

Shoes are easily removed and maybe you should invest in a pair of 'pooing' shoes.

An excellent put down for the 'peerer under the door' type person would be (for a man) to don a pair of high heels with some short leg black tights, and a pair of army boots for the girls.

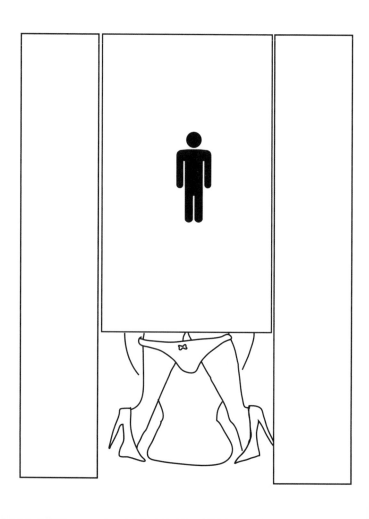

The Hollywood Solutions!

The Problem (men only):
It happens to us all – we use the urinal and a worrying fart informs us we need a poo. However, one of the other cubicles is taken and for some reason, we don't want its occupant to know that we intend to move from the urinal to the more serious part, the business end, of the loo. It's just one of those things!

Wash your hands, leave the toilet and return as a different character. That's right – all you have to do is invent a different walk so they don't recognise the sound and tempo of your shoes… yes, be a thespian darling!

"The Stalls Are Alive With the Sound of Pooing!"

Yes, the toilet can be a veritable 'Top of the Plops' with its weird and wonderful collection of sounds.

'The Sound of Poosic' brings in a host of toilet entertainment.

We could talk about 'Later, With Poos Holland', 'The Shitman and Her' and 'The Shart Show', 'Mrs. Brownies Boys' and 'The log on the Starship Enterprise', 'Dr Poo', 'The 9 o'clock Poos', 'Poo's night', 'SaTURDay night live', among other contenders

TOILETIQUETTE
THE F.A.Q'S

Q: If I know it's going be a big, painful, over baked delivery, is it acceptable to say a little prayer out loud before commencing?

A: Definitely! Toileting can be a very spiritual act.

Q: Whilst dealing with a tough one, is it OK to grunt?

A: Yes. Fellow cubicle inhabitants should respect that, for some, verbal expression can aid in the delivery process. Just try not to sound like a female tennis player!

Q: How do I stop the plop?

A: It's all about the roll in the bowl! Throw

some toilet paper down before you begin.
This is called preparing your crash mat,
a not uncommon procedure but it's quite
wasteful with the planet's finite resources.
To note, this also helps with skid mark and
splash reduction.

Q: After a successful delivery, is it ok to
celebrate?
A: This depends. Hosting a party is probably
a bad idea but a fist pump and a modest
verbal outburst would be acceptable.
However, be respectful not to taunt those
around who are yet to deliver. Remember –
this is not a competition!

Q: Is it ok to start a conversation with
someone in the next cubicle?
A: Unless it's an emergency, absolutely not.

As previously discussed in this guide, anonymity is very important to a lot of pooers.

Q: If the person in the next cubicle is wiping and I arrive at the wiping stage also, should I wait for them to finish before I start?

A: Good question! Some wipers get into a rhythm so if you start wiping at the same time, it could be a bit like a drummer playing a Metallica beat as the guitarist strums out a Westlife ballad.
This would have to be a judgement call I'm afraid!

Q: Is it ok to sing on the toilet?

A: One hundred per cent no! For some people, the ten minutes they spend on the toilet each day is the only time they get to sit in quiet reflection. Plus, most people are trying to read, and in these hallowed chambers you would very likely get 'shushed' and be asked to leave!

Q: Can I phone my girlfriend / boyfriend for a chat?

A: **NO!** Toilets are gender segregated - no gents in the ladies or vice versa, and no vice in the gents or ladies in the versa vicer.

Q: What about cleaners? Can we talk to them?

A: No. Cleaners must be, necessarily, physically and emotionally removed from their clientèle.

Cleaners are like doctors who look upon the human body as a machine (albeit a fairly dirty, poo pumping, stinky type of machine), but don't push this too far by wandering about with your bits hanging out.

Q: Can I chat up the cleaner?
A: If you must, at your convenience, but try not to talk too much old shite.

Q: If I blather the toilet, i.e. leave a great dirty old mess in there, what is the Toiletiquette? Should I; talk to the cleaner, attempt to clean it up a bit myself or, throw toilet paper around to cover it up?
A: You must always do the right thing in these circumstances.

When the coast is clear – get the hell out of there. If you meet a cleaner on the way out say, "Oh my god! Just look at what someone's done in there," and leg it.

WEE WEE

Putting the Pee in Polite

The Toiletiquette of Urinals

This section is obviously for men but some women (false moustache and baggy top and trousers) have enjoyed experimenting with a urinal. The only safe way for them to do it is to reverse up to the urinal. (Don't stand next to one of these or you might get more than you went in for).

But for most women it is a total mystery what goes on in a line of urinals. Their imagination goes into overdrive as they contemplate of a line of men stood up wagging their willies at the wall with barely a few square centimetres of privacy on either side and, in many urinals, nothing at all to separate their dignities. The secret goings on inside the urinals are

about to be revealed for the delectation of
the ladies!

But to men, of course, there is nothing unusual
or bizarre about the practice of baring all
collectively with perfect strangers, it's perfectly
natural.
But, in this slightly unnatural setting of blokes
baring bits there is a Toilettiquette in the urinal
which has to be observed to avoid confusion
and improper behaviour so that the job can
be completed with the minimum of fuss and
embarrassment.

Urinal Types

Mostly, men just walk up, pee and walk away
but there are three distinct urinal types that
stand out.

The COY type

This type is not really comfortable with the 'line up'. Often they will use the cubicle instead of slashing it out with the men of the front line. When they do step forward they angle themselves away from the others and if this is not possible, they curl their hand around their willies in such a way as to shield them from any possible prying eyes. This usually finishes up with a certain amount of wee wee on the hands. The COY type usally spend a lot of time scrubbing in the sink.

The COCKY type

This type do not care who watches. They just get on with it. They walk boldly up to the urinal and flop it out with a flourish and begin peeing almost immediately. They look around from side to side and often initiate a manly conversation, usully in a deeper tone to their normal voice to eliminate the possible misunderstanding of a chat up line. They shake it around a lot, grunt a few times, zip and stride confidently away. A style that is much envied, particularly by the COY type who is still trying to overcome his nerves to initiate his wee whilst MR. COCKY has upped and gone.

The I'VE GOT A BIG 'UN type

This type usually don't have a big one but they go through all the pretensions of having one. They march confidently to the urinal and proceed with a great flourish to unbuckle their jeans, which they leave balancing on the top of their buttocks, then pull down the front of their underpants, lean back and project a strong stream upwards giving the impression of something powerful down there. Their willies are obviously too big to pop through their underpants and zips like most mere mortals. These types go to great lengths to conceal their manhood from prying eyes and thus preserve the myth. The finish is much of the same; furious buckling and flourishing before making a swift exit.

The golden toiletiquette rule for urinals is:

Avoid peeing, if at all possible, in a trough which is immediately next to another man. Obviously, when the loo is busy and when there are only 2 urinals, this can't be much helped. The general rule is, give as much room to the other fella as you can.

If a man is on his own, peeing merrily away, in a largish, say, 10 trough urinal and you come in and plonk your percy at the porcelain right next to him. Well, suspicions as to your intentions –

trying to take a crafty peek, amorous intentions, or trying to sell him double glazing, will doubtless come to mind.

It's a bit like a draughts board really where every other space is left free.

A dilemma is where to stand when there are 3 urinals in a row, and the answer is, never in the middle! In the middle, the likelihood of a close encounter is highly possible.

Only ever choose the middle urinal or space at the trough when there are no others available!

If you do have to occupy that space, and you arrive when there is a man in full flow at each side, please refrain from using the phrase...

'...is there room for a little one?'

Eyes Down and Look In...

Curiosity is natural but please – refrain!
Keep your eyes on your own and your stream
in the bowl...

Curiosity can be very dangerous!

The Toilettiquette of Farting in the Urinal

Quite bizarrely, it is considered bad form to fart whilst taking a pee in the urinal. Walking forward, weeing, and retreating is generally done in a kind of personal, private space, even if there are many others at your side weeing merrily away. There is a quiet, unspoken dignity in the act as if you are totally alone. A fart in this hallowed atmosphere is akin to a waiter dropping a glass in a restaurant. Everyone looks in your direction. However, generally the moment is saved by humour as, for men at least, there is nothing more funny than an impromptu fart. The farter cannot remain silent at this point and needs to come up with some quip to acknowledge his malfeasance, therefore the fart is usually followed by something like, "better out than in, eh!", or "the acoustics are good in here!".

The Joker in the Stalls

There is always one who, by possibly needing to overcome his embarrassment of the silent ritual of men peeing side by side, has to crack a few funnies in the dunny.

The usual fare is on the lines of:

"Phew, just made it" followed by (now the joker plays the part of an imaginary other person in the next trough) "Can you make ME one like that!"

Ha ha. Hilarious, think the others, trying to concentrate on their flow.

This is often followed by, "wow, the pocelain's cold at the bottom" or "the water's deep" or some such jocular references to having a long penis.

It does take the boredom out of a long, sustained, beery pee but...

     ...it's never as funny as an impromptu fart!

Break a Leg...

Stage fright is very common when you're not alone at the urinal and this is nothing to be ashamed of.
Just relax and breathe... but not too heavily, that could very easily give the wrong impression!

Synchronised Bladders

We all have that one person who, like you, is taking some time to start and then they start to pee at the same time as you!
This can be a bit disconcerting but don't let it freak you out.
If necessary you will have to be ready with new and interesting conversation!

Whistle while you work?

Some men like to stamp their feet a bit before and after the act and others like to whistle. Whistling while you're pistling is totally acceptable. Just keep your whistled songs light and fun... no tear jerkers!
Singing? **Definitely NO!**

Competitive Peeing

Who can pee the longest?

Who can stand furthest away and still comfortably hit the back of the pot?

Who can pee the hardest? (you know those pees that make you think a horse has wandered in beside you).

Who can pee the highest?

(this has to go to the Duke of Edinburgh because he is the highest pee-er (peer, geddit?)

How To Poo on a First Date

It is quite natural to have nerves on a first date; he wants to impress his date with his sophistication and elegant gentlemanly manner, and she want's him to think of her as a smart intelligent, exquisite being full of fun and someone quite capable of being an entertaining and clever dinner or drinks companion.

The first fart, when one is finally able to relax in the relationship, is quite a long way down the road.

You want everything to be right. You've spent hours preparing for this. You've chosen your clothes carefully. You smell good and your hair is looking pretty cool. In fact you've been so anxious that you've completely forgotten about your necessary bodily functions and this neglect is about to catch up with you:

- In that quiet, secluded bar which he or she has suggested
- In the very exclusive restaurant
- on the sofa in her or his house

As the rumblings start you know that your body, normally your faithful friend, is about to let you down. So what are you going to do to overcome this potential catastrophe?

No Farting Aloud

You are in the restaurant. You should never have chosen an Indian on a first date. Not this Indian, anyway. Apart from the ridiculous prices there is only one tiny toilet and the best seat they could offer is right next to this. You desparately need to go for the 'full monte'. My God, why didn't you go before? Unbeknown to you, she is feeling exactly the same. The evening is going so badly as you are both in the most excruciating pain trying to hold back the mighty balloon of wind that threatens to explode and engulf the whole restaurant. And the poppadums and beer that you have both wolfed down minutes ago are beginning to exact their revenge!

"I think we should give the curried fish a miss"

Solution

Whilst her attention is diverted by the exotic looking waiter asking for her order you surreptitiously text your best mate asking him to phone you urgently.

"What, suddenly dropped dead, Oh My God. Yes, I'll just step outside", and you skip outside with your phone cradled in your ear as you tap your pockets looking for something. What you are looking for are, in fact, your car keys and you run out, jump in it and race to the pub around the corner and without even looking at the bar you march purposefully into the loo where blessed relief awaits.

Yes, you were gone a longish time but you have a perfect excuse to elaborate upon.

She, meantime, delighted at your absence, avails herself of the delights of the convenient convenience and the rest of the evening goes swimmingly well, both pleased with their own ingenuity.

Other Restaurant tips

Do not panic! Easy to say, we know, but when you're nervous and anxious, your bowels tend to misbehave even more.

What you need to do is to excuse yourself. Novices amongst us may be asking "why don't you just say you're going to the toilet?" And the answer is – time.

If you simply announce that you're using the toilet, the time you spend in there informs your date as to whether you've had a number one or a number two, a very important bit of TMI on a first date.

Here are some other ways you can excuse yourself:

• When in a restaurant, announce that you're going to use the toilet but that you're also going to check the Specials Board on your way back – just remember to actually check the specials board for a few brief seconds on your way back!

A pee + specials board is about the equivalent to a brisk, but not too leisurely, poo.

• If you can't make an excuse in advance – make one on your return. Something like – 'I saw an old family friend on my way back who kept me talking', or 'I got chatting to the chef and asked them to make everything extra special just for you, or even, 'I had to give someone the kiss of life!'.

It's probably best to make sure they don't think the last one occurred in the toilet, though!

Your Place Or Mine

The time you spend away from your date is the only real concern when you're out having drinks or enjoying a meal.

However, when you are invited back for coffee and you feel the urgent need to go – you also have the whole issue of concealing evidence! Here are some ways to make sure the only lasting impression you make on your date is your date, and not murky memories in the toilet!

• Before you leave the room, turn the TV or the music up. This will help to 'sound proof' the process.

• Before you drop anchor, make sure there's enough toilet roll (soiling a shower curtain is not the sort of first date story you'll both laugh about in years to come!)

• As per earlier advice, create your crash mat in the bowl to help reduce noise, splash-back and skid-marking!

• Make a pre-emptive flush! This is very important. In the modern era of toilet rolls so thick they could keep you warm in the arctic for days, the risk of blocking the toilet has never been greater.

Think about it. With your nice new date outside, in terms of nightmares on the WTDRHRN scale (I want to die right here, right now), this would be number one.

• Mask the scent. Spray if you can find something to spray with. Use any toiletry product you can find to flush out the loo but, dont use shampoo as the bubbles will follow you into the lounge after flushing.

Unless you have a soulmate with no sense of smell and who is hard of hearing you will continually be plagued with the constant dating and farting syndrome.

Perhaps deep underground somewhere, the world's greatest geniuses are working on a solution to the whole 'dating vs farting' situation and one day, they will rid us of this often painful and frequently embarrassing predicament!

Until that day, you may have to make do with some of the following suggestions...

Cork

This is a bit drastic but a cork up the backside can contain a decent quantity of farts for a reasonable amount of time.

However, choose your cork carefully. A champagne cork is designed to retain powerful gasses but the laws of physics may trump this ingenuity and the cork may 'report', firing out and ripping through your underwear, bringing all manner of unwanted detritus with it and waking up whole neighbourhoods with a crack like the backfire of a 500 Yamaha with a broken silencer.

Not for the faint hearted (or the 'aint farted').

It's A WIND Up

Use any means to divert blame from yourself

When out walking with your new love, hang behind to tie your shoelaces and sneakily let one go. Beware a change of wind direction may mean that your rumblings might be rumbled. If you are passing some industrial complex (preferably sewage treatment or a gasworks) you might remark that they often work overtime at this hour.

Using a Scapegoat
(or scapedog in this instance)

If all else fails blame the poor unfortunate, faithful mutt who lovingly stands close to you both, prepared to take the blame for all your misdemeanours.

But beware, it may come back to bite you on the bum (deservedly) as the dog is quite capable of creating a stink of his own, and you might well get the blame for that!

Toileting Abroad
Curling One Out in Another Culture

Us Brits are a funny old lot and our bowels are no different. It would seem that as soon as they leave British air space, they experience a home sickness that manifests itself into what can only be described as a series of dirty protests. Yes, we've all of us very nearly soiled our shorts around the pool, crapped our kecks in a café or babbed our pants on the beach, and often, all before breakfast.

One of the reasons may well be the good old language barrier. By the time we've asked one of our continental cousins 'Where's the bog' in English with a dodgy, foreign accent 20 times - what started out as subtle twinge in the bowels has escalated into a contorted colon on the brink of catastrophe.

To that end, here are some useful phrases

in some of the more common international languages we encounter on holiday:

• "Excuse me, where is the nearest toilet?"
  IN FRENCH: Excusez moi, Ou est le plus proche des toilettes?

• "Quickly – where is the toilet as I am about to fire faecal matter into the lining of my underpants?"
IN SPANISH: Rápidamente! ¿dónde está el baño? como estoy a punto de disparar la material fecal en el forro de mis calzoncillos.

• "Can you please contact the British embassy and let them know that I need relief ... I have passed solids in my underpants?"
IN GERMAN: Können Sie bitte an die Britische Botschaft und informieren sie, dass

ich Nothilfe brauchen … Ich habe Feststoffe
in meiner Unterhose weitergegeben.

• "Do you sell British underpants?"
  IN ITALIAN: Vendete mutande britannici?

• "Is it really necessary for me to throw my
  toilet roll in the bin?"
  IN GREEK: Είναι πραγματικά απαραίτητο
  για μένα να ρίξει ρολό τουαλέτας μου στον
  κάλαθο των αχρήστων;

• "Really? Are you sure?"
  IN GREEK: Αλήθεια; Είσαι σίγουρος;

• "Excuse me – Can you teach me insulting
  words in your language so I can swear to you
  about the state of my hotel room toilet?"
  IN DUTCH: Pardon - Kunt u me leren

beledigende woorden in uw taal, zodat ik zweer het je over de staat van mijn hotelkamer wc?

- "Do you allow English people to use your safe and hygienic toilet facilities (or are we not quite there yet in our international relations)?"
IN SCOTTISH: Doooo ya allow thoose devils from ooover the burder to use your seafe and hygeeeenic bogs (or am I beeeing reeediculooos?)

The Toilettiquette of Using a Continental Squatter

Firstly, you must avoid these things like a dose of diarrhoea. They are not meant for humans. Some say that it produces the most natural squatting position but in comfort terms, they are the pits (literally!).

These ghastly contraptions are impossible to clean and the smell of a Frenchman's lavabo is not easily forgotten.

However, if you are forced (by your stupidity in travelling to primitive places) to use one of these abominations, then, in order to avoid losing all your prized, pocket possessions you must observe the Toiletiquette of the squatter. This mainly applies to men who, in the absence of a 'man bag', will cram their pockets with all manner of unsuitable things; bottle openers, food, hip flasks, energy drink, condoms, as well as the essentials; keys, wallet, smartphone and half a kilo of loose change.

There is only one thing to do. Remove these items steadily in the limited confines of the crappatarium, creating a serious risk of your treasures dropping down the bottomless pit or, you can go bottomless yourself. In other words, strip off for the act. The only safe way is to remove everything, completely 'bollocky-buff'. Thus suitably dis-attired, you can poo away to your heart's content, safely, in the knowledge that the only thing that will fall down the trap is what you went in for and if you soil yourself – then your clothes are safe from that as well!

Book Reading on a Continental Squatter

Yes. Can be done but usually these places are very dark, - the miserly, money saving switch having gone out long before you get your pants down. If you must read, and for some this is necessary to give thrusting inspiration, then first put your book, open at the appropriate page, into a re-sealable plastic bag because it will almost certainly end up down there in the slime. If you're lucky enough to fish it out, then after you have incinerated the re-sealable plastic bag, it will be as good as new.

Hard Times Toileting

It's considered a crime by some.
To leave without wiping your bum.
But there's times when it has to be done –
so carry it off with aplomb!

(we changed the last line in the interests of propriety from: **so get busy with your thumb!**)

Toilettiquette Allows You To Flush And Go If...

...you have done the dirty deed and you suddenly discover to your horror that, in your chosen cubicle, there is no paper. In this scenario you must re-locate, wherever possible, to another, better equipped cubicle.

This will involve a kind of knee-knocked shuffle (to keep the minimum contact between unclean bum and underwear) as you search frantically for salvation.

If you are unlucky, you may have to do the silly walk for some time until you find what you are looking for (or until natural evaporation takes over and leaves you with a crusty behind!)

Not Wiping's The Right Thing If...

...you are caught short in the wild and the surrounding foliage is a less than a suitable replacement for toilet roll.

Constipation

Constipation is not nice. It takes away all the pleasures associate with a satisfying poo, it can make one miserable and it can hurt. It's often caused by dietary issues or just the body's inability to process waste in a normal cyclical manner, on a daily basis.

We shouldn't make light of this unpleasant experience, - but we will!

It is important to eat and drink wisely to relieve the misery of a protracted period on the pot where very little occurs therefore we have our recommendations.

There is very little that cannot be moved next morning in the wee room of the house after copious quantities of Guinness followed by an unbearably hot curry. Our personal recommendation is 5 pints of the black stuff followed by a rich vindaloo. Avoid naan breads and stodgy stuff like that and stick to the rice. Next morning it may not be a pleasing experience, the stench could be overpowering and your bottom could experience several degrees of dangerous burning (maybe advisable to put the toilet roll in the fridge the night before) but your hitherto reluctant parcel for delivery will fire out like a champagne cork at a Grand Prix gathering!

How To Solve a Problem Like Diarrhoea?

Diarrhoea is an emergency state and as such, much of the standard toiletiquette can be suspended as body and soul is put asunder in an effort to combat the problem.

Let's face it, it's less about adhering to toilettiquette and more about avoiding soiled kecks!

There are some splendid 'blockers' on the market such as immoodiunum, or something like that and we should treat this subject with the respect and decency it deserves.

But we won't!

Again it is down to eating and drinking to solve the problem. Our recommendation is:

5 pints of Guinness followed by an unbearably hot vindaloo.

This will kill off all the germs in your gut but, importantly, your next morning experience in the toilet will prove to be little different, with all the similar symptoms, whether you still have a dose of diarrhoea or not.

Our final recommendation, if all the above fails, is to wear a pair of baggy trousers and apply bicycle clips to both ankles!

Conversations Gone Potty!

Life these days is frantically busy - so much so that when we're not working overtime to pay for the latest gadget, (that we must have, but will never use) we're at home cooking Jamie Oliver recipes or blindly recycling all the rubbish that comes through the door (such as energy bills, rent reminders, more rent reminders, final rent reminders and eviction notices etc, etc). The thing is, with all these things to do – we barely get time to have a proper conversation with our loved ones. However, the modern family being the ever evolving phenomenon that it is has found a pocket of time during which the whole family can fill each other in on the day's events.

And this time is... toilet time!

Talking through the Toilet Door

Yes, many a family conversation these days will take place through the toilet door. A couple, for instance, may arrive home in the evening and go upstairs to get changed before making (or ordering!) dinner. As one is in the bathroom, the other will often be in a nearby bedroom getting changed or wiping the dribble from their shoulder courtesy of a sleeping 'seat buddy' on the bus. Therefore, in a bid to actually communicate with each other on an evening, a couple will often pursue a conversation through the toilet door.

Sure, the acoustics in the bathroom aren't

great and the inhabitant has to shout a bit
but if you're prepared to put up with the odd
'pushing' related pause from the one on the pot
– it can be a worthwhile endeavour and a vital
aid in relationship communications.

Potential Issues With Talking Through The Toilet Door:

• Sound effects – when it comes to
communicating through the toilet door,
you might get a little more sound than you
bargained for. As well as being graced with a
story about how your partner managed to get
some free chocolate drops from the vending
machine at work, you may also be the 'not
so proud' recipient of some chocolate plops
yourself, as well as the pre and post poo wind,
and of course – the grunts, groans and general
tap bending of the person who should

probably consider increasing their fibre intake!

"How's your day been?"
"Oh, pretty crappy, how about you?"

• Fragrance – whilst toilet doors do their best to provide a decent barrier between a fresh and pungent dump, and the sweet air on the other side where the rest of the world can breathe freely – they can only do so much.

Poo is a potent force and its fragrance is keener than the mustard that helped to flavour it. It can definitely travel under doors and through keyholes and if your door is pretty thin – it may even make its way through that too!

• Muffling and reverb – it's true that with their natural reverb and gentle echo, bathroom acoustics make Dad's singing sound just like Frank Sinatra (according to Dad). However, when it comes to speaking to somebody beyond the confines of a closed bathroom door – these chaps can sometimes be the roguish little agents of mischief.

Innocent phrases such as "I'd love a bit of ham and pickle" can potentially be misheard as being "I'd love a bit of slap and tickle."

Now, slap and tickle in the bathroom, mid poo, is a whole new world of toiletiquette, not to mention health and safety!

Open Door Policy

In order to avoid the above complications but still maintain a conversation, some people will employ an 'open door policy' when it comes to using the toilet. The first thing to point out is the fact that this completely removes any barrier when it comes to preventing the spread of poo smell which, it has to be said, carries a few health and safety concerns as well as raising questions of decency! So whilst it might improve the acoustics of a toilet based conversation, it may, in the same breath, engender a very inconvenient need to vomit on your partner and stink the house out to the extent that you have to go to the neighbours for tea!

Only for the most liberal minded!

The 'No Choice' Communications Through the Toilet Door

No matter how reserved or particular you are when it comes to talking through the toilet door, there will always be occasions when talking or shouting to a partner or family member is essential.

"Darling - I've found the missing Anaconda from number 42!"

Here are some examples:
"Mum! Mum! Mum! MUM! MUM! MUM! MUM!"
"What?"
"Can you bring some toilet paper up please?"

"Barry!"
"Yes, love?"
"How many times have I told you to put the toilet seat down?"
"I always put the toilet seat down, honey."
"If that's the case; please explain why I am currently sat in the toilet, rather than on it?!"

"Darling! Can you call a plumber out please? I've got my arm stuck in the U-bend again."

"Honey! Can you fetch the mop and bucket asap? I forgot to courtesy flush halfway through and I was using that extra quilted toilet paper you bought!"

"Sweetheart! Can you please fetch me some new underpants from the bedroom and please don't ask any questions?"

"Honey! Don't run any water! I'm going to have to get straight in the shower... it's up my back!"

"Mum! Can you come and clean my finger? I didn't realise this toilet paper was so thin!"

So What's the Toiletiquette When it Comes to Talking Through the Toilet Door?

The first thing to say is that partaking in this activity is first and foremost a judgement call. If you think your relationships can withstand the potential problems associated with this means of communication then knock yourselves out.

However, if you're the sort of people who are particularly sensitive to the sounds and scents of the baser side of life – then pursuing this endeavour may actually result in you literally knocking yourselves out!

Is Toilet Talk Taboo?

This question that has pervaded society since humanity's first ever offering. You won't be surprised to learn that here at HQ, we're very open when it comes to this subject – so much so that we have a monthly Toilet Talk Seminar, attended by every member of staff (which serves to create a very crowded toilet cubicle, we really should move those gatherings to a meeting room!). Therefore, our opinion is that poo is a perfectly acceptable subject for public consumption, if you pardon the expression. However, not everybody is of the same opinion and as such, their views should be respected. The point here is to know your audience as let's face it, the demure, elderly lady you sit next to on the bus may not be the best candidate for a discussion about the length of your skid marks!

The Toiletiquette of Toilet Talk

If you do find somebody who shares your openness to talking all things toilet, then that's great but it's worth taking on board a few notes about the toiletiquette of these kinds of relations:

1. **Toileting is not a competition:**

Any conversations about size, length of time, number of people you can make throw up with smell etc should not be converted into a competition. Toileteers should be a bohemian, hippy-esque society of people willing to share for sharing's sake who look out for their brothers and sisters. That said, we're still undecided as to whether or not the launch of Crudstock (the toilet equivalent of Woodstock) is a great idea…

2. **Be True to your Poo:**

When it comes to conversations about anything in life, many of us are prone to the occasional exaggeration. However, if you want to truly reap the benefits of a good old toilet talk, you have to be true to your poo. Be as accurate as you can when it comes to frequency, size and consistency and whatever you do, don't adopt the mores of a wine expert when it comes to describing your scent – "It has the woody wistfulness of forgotten cauliflower and the whirling whisper of an eastern banquet!"

3. **Be Careful What You Pick Up:**

Whilst this is always good advice when it comes to any facet of toileting, in the context of toilet talk it relates to the picking up of bad habits.

Just because your best mate can't be bothered wiping, it doesn't mean you should do the same - and you should definitely never offer to do his or her laundry!

4. **Be Mindful of Those Close by:**
Whilst we're all for talking toilet in similar minded company – we'd also like to think that we're respectful of those who are of a non-toilet talk persuasion. To that end, we would suggest that when you are engaging in one of these largely fruitful (and fibre-full) discussions, you consider if the conversation is likely to upset those in close proximity to you. It isn't, for example, a good idea to talk diarrhoea down the local cafe as poor old Mrs Prude takes in her first mouthful of the chef's special beef broth!

Pooing Away From Home

In a lot of ways, pooing is a lot like football. It can last about the same amount of time, carry a range of dangerous fouls and like every footballer, a pooer always prefers performing at home. However, like footballers, pooers have to be professional enough to produce the goods when away from the sanctuary of their home stadium/bathroom.

Yes, whether it's at your Grandma's, your best friend's or your partner's house – you need to know how to conduct yourself on unfamiliar porcelain. So, as you will have guessed, with pooing away from home comes a number of toiletiquette points.

And some of these are:

• Leave the toilet the way it was before you used it –

Now, this may seem impossible as without the use of air freshener, you probably think there's little you can do about the smell. This is naïve. As soon as you've plopped – give the toilet a flush. This gets rid of the smell producing article as quickly as possible and thus gives you the best chance of reducing the smell you leave behind.

Other things to consider are to throw 'roll in the bowl' before you go (to reduce splash back and skid marks – as previously mentioned in this book), try your best not to break the toilet seat and if you're a bloke – wipe away those nasty little drips from the rim of the bowl (you know what we're talking about!)

• **Keep the Floodgates Closed –**
This is one of the points that pops up a few times in this book and that is because it is so essential – courtesy flush, courtesy flush, COURTESY FLUSH! The last thing that's going to impress your new girlfriend's or boyfriend's parents is you turning their staircase

into a very alternative, and not very appealing, Log Flume!

• **Always Wash Your Hands –**
Obvious health and safety concerns aside, leaving your mark on your in-laws really shouldn't be something they have to wipe from their palm following a handshake.

• **The post poo re-entry into the living room –**
There are four main schools of thought here. The **first** is to be honest and announce to people that you have a healthy and regular bowel and that you are happy to report this has just been evacuated bang on schedule.
The **second** is to walk in and pretend that absolutely nothing has happened at all. This will require for you to act like you don't know

what people are talking about when they say things like **"we thought you'd fallen in."** The **third** approach is to make a pre-emptive comedy strike which involves you delivering a self-swiping quip as soon as you re-enter the social group – something along the lines of, "I feel a stone lighter after that!", "Give it a few minutes before you go in there!", "Don't go in there without a canary!" (old miner's joke) The **fourth** approach is not recommended. This approach involves the fabrication of an elaborate lie that attempts to explain your protracted absence. Excuses such as, "Whilst I was in the bathroom, an injured bird came in through the window so I've spent the last ninety minutes fixing its wing and helping it to fly again." Really don't wash – especially when you've used a bathroom with no window!'

Toileting on the Go –
The Moving Target!

Much of this book has looked at using the toilet in a home or out in public but there is another venue for your bottom based performance – the moving vehicle. We are primarily thinking of those vehicles that are actually equipped for toileting, such as the train, the coach or the plane. (however, She-wee's and He-wee's are now becoming more common for use in the car, but you're not supposed to do it while you are driving!)

When using any of these fast moving facilities, the first piece of advice is to always follow the guidelines as to when they can and can't be used. We're not exactly sure why they have such restrictions but let's face it – nobody wants to find out the hard/embarrassing way!

Other considerations include –

- **Balance** – This one's primarily for the men. If any women reading this thought their other half's aim was bad in the house bathroom – you should see it in a moving vehicle! So when a man goes for a wee on a moving vehicle, he needs to consider the fact that there are two main goals he is trying to achieve. The first is to get his stream in the bowl (as opposed to on the floor, the walls and the ceiling!) and the second is to stay on his feet. Achieving both can be difficult. One tactic to consider is the deployment of the 'no hands' approach to weeing. This basically entails getting the little man out and then removing your hands from the operation all together. The benefit of this approach is the fact that you can then use your hands to maintain your balance by either placing them on the walls or holding onto something.
- **Causing a Stink** – Some coach

manufacturers make the sensible decision to place their vehicle toilet in a kind of downstairs compartment out of the way. However, some don't. The problem with the latter is that it creates a situation whereby a toilet is placed in close proximity to seating *(I think you can see where this is going)*. Naturally, these seats are avoided by the first waves of passengers to board the coach but when it comes to those really popular journeys – some poor passengers really do end up with the proverbial end of the stick!

• **The Mr Whippy Effect –** Sitting down to deliver the goods on a moving vehicle has potential to produce the rare yet often referenced, Mr Whippy poo. This is where the agent of delivery (the bum) is moved in a circular motion as the operation is conducted.

The only advice we have here is to resist putting a flake in it!

"Anyone care for dessert"

• **Road Blocks –** It's bad enough being stuck in traffic on the M1 without the coach being flooded with the mashed up remains of your attempt to bankrupt a Chinese 'all you can eat' buffet the night before. So our final plea is simple – **DON'T BLOCK THE TOILET!**

Poops, I did it Again!

We've previously touched on the whole dating vs farting thing in this book but what we haven't discussed is how to deal with **farts that aren't your own**.

Farts that aren't your own are a common problem. They can occur on a bus, in a pub and even at charity events! We have, in this guide, attempted to provide theories as to how to deal with the need to fart yourself and when it comes to one's own farts most adults have also developed their own techniques in dealing with their inconvenient nature.

However, one thing we have never even got close to mastering is the ways in which we should deal with farts committed by other people.

At the bottom of all this are two facts – the first is that the sound of someone else's fart is funny, and the second is the fact that the smell of somebody else's fart is quite simply stomach turning.

Especially those ones where you can have a good guess at the person's diet the day before!
Yuk!

So, what is the toiletiquette when it comes to other people's farts I hear you cry? (over the sound of somebody farting at book writing HQ ... I think they had cabbage for tea!)

Well, there is no 'one size fits all farts' solution, so we think the best thing to do is to give you a couple of examples of potentially awkward 'other person's' fart scenarios. **(Also known as rogue farts, wrong side of the bed farts or which dirty fekker did that farts.)**

What to do When Your Date Accidentally Farts:

If you're a bloke and your female date has farted, the gentlemanly thing to do is to try your best to act as though you neither heard it, nor smelt it. So, the first thing to do is not react. This sounds impossible but if you think about it, when your nose detects a fart, there is usually a couple of seconds gap before your response of 'Urghhh!' or 'Whose is THAT?' is propelled from your mouth.

If, however, the fart has both the decibels and the depth to warrant a place in the local brass band, then pretending you didn't hear this *'fartophony'* can pose quite a problem.

You can try and say something like, 'This sofa

makes odd noises' or 'Next door's telly's loud' but as valiant as these efforts would be, you will not spare your fair maiden's blushes. However, such attempts may get you points for gentlemanly conduct.

If the fart is both loud and horrendously smelly though – then laughter may be your only option. (There are very few men who can contain the mirth that a great fart brings, so this will be easy).
You will just have to hope she sees the funny side too!

On the flip side, if you're a woman and your male date farts – you have the right to chastise him by whatever legal means you deem appropriate. No bloke should fart in front of a woman until at least the third date!

Work Based Belters

The work place is a strange and varied arena for the humble old fart and this makes the Toiletiquette for work place wind breaks both variable and relative. If you work on a building site for example, then you would probably be more concerned and upset if you had a colleague who didn't regularly throw out a bum tune or two. However, if you work in an office, it is always a massive thing when somebody farts. If it is a bloke, he will find himself in the conflicted position of wanting his male work pals to smell the fart and provide feedback at the same time as wanting to remain anonymous where female colleagues are concerned. The Toiletiqeutte for blokes is to never grass another bloke up as, just like a really good fart – what goes around, comes around!

The Phantom Farter

We've all had that moment chatting to someone in the supermarket and then suddenly, out of nowhere, a smell envelops you so strong it makes you want to choke. The first thing you tend to do in this situation is to double check with your brain that you are not the source (let's face it – we will all often quite honestly answer the question 'Have you farted?' with the answer 'I'm not sure!')

However, your brain quickly reassures you that the offending gust is not your 'tang' so your attention turns the other suspect – the person with whom you are in close conversation. Before even thinking about asking them, your first tactic is to study their face for any tell-tale signs of guilt. Such signs might include a blush of embarrassment, a wry smile or movement that indicates a full pair of underpants. When none of these signs are present, you will often enjoy the temporary relief of knowing it is neither you nor your companion who has violated the air you are sharing. This relief however is short lived as your mind then entertains the possibility that your companion may themselves be in the process of studying you for any telltale signs of guilt. This possibility produces a worry that you don't look innocent which thus causes you to make an effort to act naturally – which is of course, unnatural.

It's at this point that you toy with the notion of acknowledging the smell in such a way as to attribute it to a third party by saying something along the lines of, 'I think someone's dumped one on us and ran!' However, before you've even had chance to purse your lips into a

speaking position you remember that old
playground adage of 'They who smelt it,
dealt it!' and you decide to remain silent.
This purposeful silence is usually the point at
which you realise that neither you nor your
companion has spoken for the duration of
the smells presence. Furthermore, after the
palpable awkwardness of your mutual inner
turmoil, you both acknowledge the fact that,
like the smell that caused this whole charade,
the mood has passed.

With a certain amount of deflation, you will
part company with a simple, 'See you' and 'All
the Best', never to discover who was, in fact...

...The Phantom Farter!

Why Does Everyone Like the Smell of their Own Trumps?

This is a question for which we can't provide an answer but we're more than happy to propose a theory. Pride is frowned upon in some circles and deemed to be a kind of man made evil – but when it comes to farts, it could be argued that it is innate. When you have a really good fart (and by that we mean one that feels great at the point of exit, is acoustically majestic and carries a scent as rich and sophisticated as an exotic wine) you feel utterly, utterly proud. Whatever else you do in life, a fart will always be yours. The pride is nothing to be ashamed of. However, what we don't recommend is the development of an unhealthy relationship with your own farts. Remember – farts are made up of potentially harmful gasses so if you go overboard on your own brand – it could be an overdose of very dangerous and very embarrassing proportions!

Our Final Farting Shot

Well, we hope that this guide has been useful and will leave you flushed with success when it comes to the subtleties and niceties of toiletiquette.

But before we parp company, we'd like to share one last sentiment that as a poo lover, we hope you'll enjoy …

Ode to Poo

Sometimes your timing's not great,

Like before I set off, when I'm late,

But I'd rather be tardy for dates,

Than risk having you, over-baked.

You're the part of my day set aside,

For true peace when in loo, I abide,

And no matter how painful or stinking,

It's with you that I do all my thinking.